Jasper
Johns

By Roberta Bernstein

RIZZOLI ART SERIES

Series Editor: Norma Broude

Jasper
Johns
(b.1930)

"At every point in nature there is something to see. My work contains similar possibilities for the changing focus of the eye. . . . Generally, I am opposed to painting which is concerned with conceptions of simplicity. Everything looks very busy to me." —Jasper Johns (*Sixteen Americans*: The Museum of Modern Art, New York, 1959)

JOHNS'S statement about the "changing focus of the eye" provides a key to understanding how profoundly his art is rooted both in the richness and the uncertainty of visual experience. The vitality of his art over the past four decades results from his continued exploration of the sensory and psychological aspects of perception.

Since the mid-1960s Jasper Johns has been recognized as one of the most important and influential artists of his generation. His earliest works, from the mid-1950s, were so blatantly representational and impersonal-looking that his art was immediately seen as making a clean break from the prevailing avant-garde style of Abstract Expressionism. His paintings and sculptures depicting common objects, signs, and words inspired new directions that emerged during the 1960s, including Pop, Minimal, Conceptual, and Process Art. Since 1954 he has produced close to 285 paintings and an extensive output of graphics. Johns's prints and drawings have become increasingly influential in his work as a way to reexamine imagery developed initially in paintings and sculptures. One of the most consistent and unique features of Johns's art has been the way he reworks imagery by changing format or color and by recombining motifs. The sense of continuity provided by this reprocessing is disrupted by his periodic introduction of unexpected new images.

I. *Flag* (1954–1955)–*Painted Bronze* (1960)

Johns has said that from age five he wanted to be an artist. He was born in 1930 and raised in South Carolina. After spending three semesters at the University of South Carolina, he moved to New York City in 1949 to study art. He served in the U.S. Army for a year and a half and was stationed in Japan for part of his service. He returned to New York in 1952 and began his first Flag painting in 1954. His first solo exhibition was held in 1958 at the Leo Castelli Gallery, where he has shown new work ever since. In a statement from 1959, Johns acknowledged Paul Cézanne (and Cubism), Marcel Duchamp, and Leonardo da Vinci as important influences on his art.

Johns's art has emerged from his upbringing in the South in the 1930s and 1940s and his artistic coming-of-age in New York City in the 1950s. He has said that he views all art making as a heroic enterprise and sees the artist as an outsider. At the same time, Johns has rejected the self-aggrandizing mythology that had become identified with modern art when he entered the cultural avant-garde during the height of Abstract Expressionism. Central to the formulation of his artistic vision was the need to separate himself from the focus on the self that was so much a part of the Surrealist and Expressionist directions in twentieth-century art. The influence and friendship of artist Robert Rauschenberg, composer John Cage, and choreographer Merce Cunningham were significant in steering Johns toward questioning established canons of art and challenging distinctions between art and life. The art-life issue, specifically as it built upon Cubism and Dada, continues to inspire Johns's work as it does much of the art of the last half-century.

From 1954 to 1960 Johns developed a repertory of images composed of flags, targets, numbers, maps, light bulbs, ale cans, and other familiar objects. He characterized them as "things the mind already knows" because they were all commonplace objects in American culture. Presenting these familiar things in the context of art allowed them to function in unexpected ways and "on other levels," as Johns described it. He specifically chose things that focus attention on the nature of art as a means of inquiry into how the eye and mind perceive reality. His paintings of flat objects, beginning with the American flag (plate 1), allowed him to depict objects while rejecting conventions of illusionist art. In order to emphasize the painting itself as object, Johns accentuated the canvas-on-stretcher construction and textured surface. Flatness is just one of many properties of these subjects that enabled Johns to begin his lifelong inquiry into the relationship between art and reality. His commitment to this concern, set forth with such clarity and conviction in these early works, is central to his idea that one of the main functions of art is to present a situation in which perceptions—coaxed from their engrained habits—have the possibility to change.

Johns has said that he dreamt one night of painting an American flag and immediately proceeded to do so. Since 1955 he has done numerous versions of flags in every medium he has worked in. His persistent reworking of this image suggests that deeply rooted personal meanings as well as pictorial qualities may keep drawing him to it. However, because the flag is a familiar cultural symbol, specific personal meanings remain hidden. It was important to Johns at this time that his subjects did not bear traces of his own personality. He also chose to deflect or restrain any political or psychological responses that might be evoked by the flag or the other objects, signs, or words that he used during this first phase. He did this by the impersonal manner in which he presented them, using the simplest or most obvious formats, such as symmetrical or serial compositions, and choosing schematic colors (usually red, yellow, and blue) or neutral monochrome (usually white or gray). Even the provocative plaster casts of anatomical fragments in his first Target paintings (plate 2) are to some extent neutralized by the way they are displayed like color-coded objects on shelves. Numbers (plate 3), letters, and words are always printed with stencils that disallow any sense of personal signature.

Similarly his Map paintings never imply personal attachments to one location over another.

In other paintings from the 1950s, Johns incorporated common household and studio objects. Such works as *Canvas* (1956), *Drawer* (1957), *Newspaper* (1957), *Coat Hanger* (1958), *Thermometer* (1959), and *Shade* (1959) focus on properties that define paintings: shape, space, texture, line, color, and surface. Johns also made sculptures that raise similar conceptual issues about art and reality. As in the Flag and Target paintings, familiar things are presented— light bulbs, flashlights, ale cans, and paintbrushes—that at first look like the thing itself, but upon closer inspection are seen to be fabricated from Sculp-Metal, plaster, bronze, and other art materials. His Painted Bronzes of 1960 (plate 6) come closest to being "fool-the-eye" images and provoke the unsettling psychological reaction that occurs when what is taken for granted is cast into doubt. These early paintings and sculptures were not solipsistic, formalist exercises, but rather profound inquiries into the nature of art, close in spirit to Ludwig Wittgenstein's rigorous philosophical investigations into the function and meaning of language. In the next phase of his art, as Johns moved openly into psychological territory, he developed a more complex pictorial language and his work became more personal and expressive.

II. *False Start* (1959)–*Decoy* (1971)

Johns's first major retrospective was held in 1964 in London and New York. In 1960 he made his first lithographs at Tatyana Grosman's Universal Limited Art Editions; since then he has made over 250 prints in various media. Johns continued to live in New York during the 1960s; in 1961 he bought a house in Edisto, South Carolina, where he lived for part of each year until it was destroyed by fire in 1966. He made his first trip to Europe in 1961 on the occasion of an exhibition of his work in Paris, and he traveled to Japan in 1964 and 1966. In 1967 he became artistic adviser to the Merce Cunningham Dance Company and designed costumes and sets for several of the company's productions through 1978.

False Start (plate 4) was a pivotal work for Johns, one in which new stylistic directions emerged and in which, according to Johns, "the object is put in even greater doubt." For the first time he used a title that is not straightforwardly descriptive and is actually acutely ironic for a work so full of new ideas. The gestural brushwork and complex color scheme create a kind of spatial ambiguity that was not found in his previous paintings, in which surfaces layered with tight brush strokes and solid planes of color were literal and flat. While he had used letters, numbers, and words before, language became a major focus of his art during the 1960s. In *False Start*, Johns printed the names of the colors that appear in the painting, adding a conceptual dimension to the sensuously painted surface. He set up ambivalent relationships between colors and words to confuse and therefore question what the eye and mind perceive as "true" and "false." The resulting lack of certainty as to how the mind attaches meaning to what the senses perceive is central to Johns's artistic endeavor. It is this quality of uncertainty that makes his art so elusive and specific meanings impossible to pin down. Yet this aura of doubt

1. *Skin with O'Hara Poem.* 1963–1965.
Lithograph, printed in black, composition, 21 × 33¹/₆".
Collection of The Museum of Modern Art, New York.
Gift of the Celeste and Armand Bartos Foundation

and ambiguity does not result in denying access, but instead invites the viewer's response.

After *False Start*, Johns integrated the visual and mental aspects of perception with the emotional. The space in Johns's works is more ambivalent and illusory, yet never straightforwardly illusionistic. The self-containment and fixed structure of his earlier work were replaced by compositions that suggest incompleteness and a breakdown of order. Yet Johns remains committed to the idea of the painting as a concrete object. Nowhere has he more effectively undermined the notion of the painting as a "window" to reality than in *Painting with Two Balls* (plate 5), in which he pried open the surface to reveal the wall on which the painting hangs. This grounding in the objectness of the artwork became increasingly important to Johns as his art shifted to a new range of subjects and new modes of presenting his imagery. His manner of applying paint and attaching objects to surfaces became more varied. Brooms, cans, rags, squeegees, stretcher bars, irons, and wire screens were used as tools for imprinting, rubbing, or scraping surfaces; assemblages of objects were fastened with hinges, wingnuts, wires, and magnets and are suspended so that they are movable or imply movement.

The intense concentration on a single or repeated object, word, or self-contained system that characterizes Johns's works until *False Start* evolved into imagery in which many varied elements play off of one another. The mood of his work changed from the emotionally removed stance of his Flags, Targets, and Numbers to the reserved, but powerfully emotive tone of a group of works from 1961, whose titles alone convey feelings of anger and loss: *Liar*, *No*, *In Memory of My Feelings*, and *Painting Bitten by a Man*. The human figure, absent from Johns's art since the 1955 *Targets*, was reintroduced during the 1960s in the form of imprints of body parts (including skulls) and casts of body fragments that evoke an expressive, often disturbing, human presence. The imprints and casts of Johns's own face, hands, feet, and torso can be interpreted as self-portraits, but their identity is always left ambiguous (plate 7 and fig. 1). The wax cast fragment of an upside-down seated figure, which may stand for the spectator/critic, first appeared in *Watchman* (fig. 2) and became an important motif in a series of paintings and related prints until its final appearance in *Decoy* (plate 9). Cautiously and cryptically, Johns introduced autobiographical references into his works during the 1960s, usually initials or names of people and places. Through references to

2. *Watchman.* 1964. Oil on canvas with objects, 85 × 60¼". Collection of Mr. Hiroshi Teshigahara

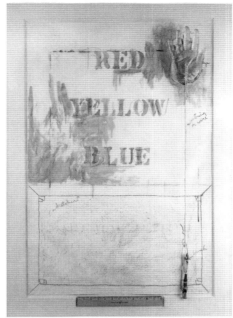

3. *Wilderness I.* 1963–1970. Charcoal, graphite, and collage on paper, 41⅛ × 26⅛". McCrory Corporation, New York

poets' names and titles and lines from poems, Johns indirectly alluded to feelings tied to his own experiences. Beginning with *Painted Bronze* (plate 6), paintbrushes and other art tools, such as rulers, stretcher bars, rags, and cans appear in many works and refer to the artist's activity in the studio (plate 8). Titles given to several of these studio pieces, such as *Wilderness I* (fig. 3), suggest the artist's anxiety during the creative process.

Throughout the work of the 1960s the names of colors are a central motif, standing for the artist's "palette" among his roster of studio tools. In many paintings, the words "Red," "Yellow," and "Blue" are printed in three horizontal registers. In works such as *Lands End* (plate 7), the letters appear to slip away from their fixed positions, to recede, reverse themselves, break apart, or float out of the picture space. In other works, including *Field Painting* (plate 8), they are aligned vertically instead of horizontally, confusing the viewer's sense of the correct orientation of the pictorial field. By the time color names appear in *Decoy* (plate 9), they have gone through many incarnations, as printed signs, as three-dimensional objects, and as photographic reproductions. Packed with references to his own paintings, sculptures, and prints, *Decoy* provides a complete summary of Johns's art since *False Start*.

III. *Untitled* (1972)–*Between the Clock and the Bed* (1981–1983)

Johns acquired a house in St. Martin, F.W.I., in 1972 and began to live and work there part of each year. In 1973 he moved to Stony Point, New York. A second major retrospective of his work was held in New York, Cologne, Paris, London, Tokyo, and San Francisco during 1977–1978. He was elected to the National Institute of Arts and Letters in 1973, received the Skowhegan Medal for Graphics in 1977, and in 1980 was elected to L'Academie Royale des Beaux Arts in Stockholm.

While *Decoy* summarizes the past, Johns's next major work, *Untitled* (plate 10), points toward the future, picking up on aspects of his art that he had not yet fully explored and spawning new directions. The wax casts show parts of

figures, mostly female and unclothed, attached to boards that crisscross the surface. The other panels are more abstract and have none of the psychologically disturbing connotations conveyed by the presentation of the human body broken into vividly realistic-looking fragments. The flagstones were inspired by a painted wall Johns saw while driving through Harlem. The pattern of stripes, or crosshatchings, came from a fleeting glimpse of a design painted on a car that passed him on the Long Island Expressway. What ties these motifs into his earlier images is that they were preexisting designs, rather than his own inventions. However, unlike his Flags, Numbers, and Maps, they could not be mechanically transferred onto the canvas, but had to be reconstructed from memory. While Johns did not include casts again in paintings until a decade later and abandoned the red, white, and black flagstone motif, he explored the imagery of this work from 1972 in many prints and drawings throughout the 1970s.

Most of Johns's paintings from the next ten years consist almost entirely of variations on the cross-hatchings that first appeared in *Untitled*. In many of these abstractions, what initially looks like continuous designs with random elements turn out to be intricate arrangements of patterns that repeat at intervals and mirror each other. In many of these, Johns employs a curious spatial effect that implies that if the surface were scrolled from side to side or top to bottom, the design would be continuous where the edges joined. Figuring out these often complicated visual puzzles demands a kind of concentration that is often contradicted by the purely sensory response evoked by Johns's virtuoso handling of encaustic, oil, lithography, monotype, watercolor, ink, and other media. In combination with the vibrant all-over pattern of the cross-hatchings design itself, the luminous surfaces and often dazzling combinations of primary and secondary color schemes create a sensuous impact.

While the painting that initiated this phase of Johns's art was untitled, the abstractions that follow have titles that add an undercurrent of expressive meaning. Some indicate references to art history: *Scent* refers to the Abstract Expressionist Jackson Pollock's last painting; *Corpse and Mirror* to the Surrealists' "Exquisite Corpse" poems and drawings; *Weeping Women* to Picasso's series of the same title; *Between*

4. *Cicada*. 1979. Watercolor and pencil on paper sheet. 38½ × 28" (sight). Collection of the artist

the Clock and the Bed to a late self-portrait by Norwegian Symbolist Edvard Munch. Other evocative titles include *Usuyuki*, meaning "thin" or "light snow," taken from a Japanese Kabuki play that Johns said "has to do with the fleeting quality of beauty in the world." *Cicada* refers to the insect that has an unusual metamorphosis from larva to adult: after living for years underground it emerges out of a shell-like casing for its short adult lifespan. In a drawing of that title (fig. 4), a band of sketches shows cicadas in different stages of their life cycle included with a skull and cross-bones, an image of fire from a book on Tantric art, and drawings after Tantric renderings of the phallus (*lingam*) and vulva (*yoni*). Taken together, these can be read as symbols of procreation, transformation, and death, themes that play an increasing role in Johns's art of the 1980s. The motifs from Tantric art that appear in *Cicada* and several other works are the first direct references to Johns's long-standing interest in Asian art and philosophy.

IV. *Perilous Night* (1982)–*Green Angel* (1990)

During this period Johns's success was further established by major exhibitions of his work in all media, awards and honors from prestigious art organizations, and record-breaking prices paid for his works. An exhibition of his work since 1974 earned him the Grand Prize at the Venice Biennale in 1988.

In 1982 an important stylistic shift occurred in Johns's art, as he moved away from his nearly obsessive reworking of the cross-hatchings that had preoccupied him during the previous decade. In two works, *Perilous Night* and *In the Studio*, Johns presented a more illusionistic space and a new range of imagery. The space that he introduced in these works is similar to still lifes in which objects hanging on walls are depicted. However, Johns does not attempt to reproduce reality in a "fool-the-eye" manner, but rather reveals the "tricks" of perception inherent in representational art. In many ways the spatial illusionism in Johns's art from this phase is closer to the Cubists' shifting viewpoints and to the Surrealists' depictions of the subconscious mind. Like

these earlier modernists, Johns is not involved with an art that mirrors reality, but one that uses a pictorial "language" to get at the truth of reality as the artist sees it. Having reached his fiftieth year, Johns revealed his preoccupation with basic issues of mortality in his art of the next decade. While these themes are not new to Johns's art, they are openly presented in complex allegories that are more explicitly autobiographical than his previous work.

The objects that Johns presents in a collage-like "screen" in *Racing Thoughts* (plate 11) are seen from the vantage point of the artist in his bathtub. In this private situation, the artist contemplates his past, present, and future as symbolized by the objects and images hanging on the wall or resting on a wicker hamper. These include a photograph of his art dealer Leo Castelli as a young man, a lithograph by Abstract Expressionist Barnett Newman, and a skull and crossbones on a Swiss sign warning of avalanches. The image of the *Mona Lisa* that Johns had used first in the 1960s suggests the importance of Leonardo da Vinci and Marcel Duchamp, who appropriated it, as long-standing artistic influences. Its centrality in the painting provides a clue to the important role images of faces play in Johns's art during this next phase. An untitled painting from 1987 (plate 12) shows women's faces depicted on three cloths. On the right is a figure called "My Wife and My Mother-in-Law" that Johns derived from a book on the psychology of perception. It is one of several perceptually ambiguous figures that can be read as two different images, a device that Johns used repeatedly during the 1980s.

The face in the center of the painting is taken from a detail of Picasso's *Straw Hat with Blue Leaf* (1936), a painting with ambiguous sexual overtones because of the erotic forms suggested by the distorted face and still-life objects. This Picasso painting, copied in full, appears in a number of Johns's works from the late 1980s, including another untitled work from 1988 (plate 15). Picasso's importance to Johns is further acknowledged in this watercolor by the double Picasso profiles stamped out by the shape of the goblet. The third face in plate 12 appears to be Johns's own invention, perhaps partly related to images of women from Picasso's Surrealist phase. Variations on the same configuration of eyes, nose, and mouth, always in the same relationship to each other and gravitating to the edges of the pictorial field, appear again and again in Johns's work. In *Montez Singing* (fig. 5), the face dominates a sparse picture space and appears with a reference to the artist's step-grandmother, Montez, one of the relatives who raised him during childhood after his parents divorced. In *Green Angel* (plate 14), the features of this same haunting face are combined with a cryptic image that may suggest one figure holding another, but whose identity remains undisclosed.

The background for the faces in plate 12 and in the left section of *Racing Thoughts* contains another image of importance to Johns during this period: the disease-ridden demon taken from Matthias Grunewald's *Isenheim Altarpiece*. This detail, extracted from Grunewald's *Temptation of Saint Anthony* panel, is divided into puzzlelike shapes and reoriented so that its identity is nearly indecipherable. The demon's association with desire and disease in Grunewald's *Temptation* scene may in part refer to the AIDS epidemic that has become so much a part of personal and public consciousness during the 1980s. Johns does not deny this association, just as he does not deny the political meanings in-

5. *Montez Singing*. 1989–1990. Oil on canvas.
76 × 50". Collection of the artist

herent in the American flag. However, he does say that these meanings did not consciously motivate his choice of either of these images and that he did not intend their meaning to lead in any one direction. What becomes increasingly apparent in Johns's art is the extent to which his subjects imply a broad range of meanings that can be taken to be both personal and cultural, as well as obvious and cryptic.

Fall (plate 13) is one of a series of four paintings, each titled after one of the seasons of the year. They suggest through the metaphor of the seasons the stages of life from childhood to old age, paralleling nature's cycle of birth, maturation, decline, and death. These are the first of Johns's works to contain a nearly complete figure, drawn from a template taken from the artist's own shadow cast on the ground. The idea for the series originated with Picasso's painting *Minotaur Moving His House* (1936), which shows the artist as minotaur moving a cart full of his possessions. The objects in the cart—the rope, ladder, canvas, and tree branch—are adopted by Johns for each work in the Seasons series. The Picasso painting provided a springboard for the artist to survey his own life and to make a broader statement on the cycle of life and the effects of the passage of time in nature. In *Fall*, the shadow is split and the artist's possessions fall apart as the ladder breaks, the rope snaps, and the canvases slide downward.

To a large extent Jasper Johns's art has been about the inevitability of change and the emotional condition of dealing with its consequences. At the same time, his art can be seen in light of the continuities that run through it. As different as his early images of familiar objects and signs may look from his recent psychologically charged allegories, there are consistent visual, conceptual, and emotional issues that connect them. From the time of his first *Flag* to his most recent work, Johns has concentrated on examining how our habits of seeing, thinking, and feeling are formed and broken. What initially appeared to be a depersonalized examination of the nature of the art object can now be seen as the beginning of a continuous commitment to exploring fundamental issues of human experience through the lens of his own life and the creative voice formed by his response to the cultural influences that have inspired him.

FURTHER READING

Armstrong, Elizabeth, James Cuno, Charles W. Haxthausen, Robert Rosenblum, John Yau, and Interview with Katrina Martin. *Jasper Johns: Printed Symbols*. Minneapolis, Minnesota: Walker Art Center, 1990.

Bernstein, Roberta. *Jasper Johns' Paintings and Sculptures: 1954–1974*. Ann Arbor, Michigan: UMI Research Press, 1985.

Bush, Andrew, John Cage, James Cuno, Richard S. Field, Fred Orton, and Richard Schiff. *Foirades/Fizzles: Echo and Illusion in the Art of Jasper Johns*. Los Angeles, California: The Grunewald Center for the Graphic Arts, Wight Art Gallery, University of California at Los Angeles, 1987.

Castleman, Riva. *Jasper Johns: A Print Retrospective*. New York: The Museum of Modern Art, 1986.

Crichton, Michael. *Jasper Johns*. New York: Abrams in association with The Whitney Museum of American Art, 1977.

Field, Richard S. *Jasper Johns Prints: 1960–1970*. The Philadelphia Museum of Art, 1970.

———. *Jasper Johns Prints: 1970–1977*. Middletown, Connecticut: Center for the Arts, Wesleyan University, 1978.

Francis, Richard. *Jasper Johns*. New York: Abbeville Press, 1984.

Geelhaar, Christian. *Jasper Johns Working Proofs*. Kunstmuseum Basel, 1979.

Kozloff, Max. *Jasper Johns*. New York: Abrams, 1969.

Rosenthal, Mark. *Jasper Johns: Work Since 1974*. Philadelphia Museum of Art, 1988.

Rosenthal, Nan, and Ruth E. Fine. *The Drawings of Jasper Johns*. Washington, D.C.: The National Gallery of Art, 1990.

Shapiro, David. *Jasper Johns Drawings: 1954–1984*. New York: Abrams, 1984.

The publisher gratefully acknowledges the generous assistance of
Leo Castelli, Robert Panzer, and Sarah Taggart.

First published in 1992 in the United States of America by
Rizzoli International Publications, Inc.
300 Park Avenue South
New York, New York 10010

Library of Congress Cataloging–in–Publication Data

Bernstein, Roberta
    Jasper Johns/Roberta Bernstein.
        p.   cm.—(Rizzoli art series)
    Includes bibliographies.
    ISBN 0–8478–1516–1
    1. Johns, Jasper, 1930–   —Criticism and interpretation.
    I. Title.   II. Series.
    N6537. J6B46   1992
    709'.2—dc20   91-45112
                                                        CIP

Series Editor: Norma Broude

Series designed by José Conde and Nicole Leong/Rizzoli

Printed in Singapore

Plates 13, 14, 15, and figs 2, 4, 5, ©Dorothy Zeidman

Complete caption information for colorplate 11:
Racing Thoughts. 1983. Encaustic and collage on canvas, 48 ×
75⅛". Collection of The Whitney Museum of American Art.
Purchase, with funds from the Burroughs Wellcome Purchase
Fund; Leo Castelli; the Wilfred P. and Rose J. Cohen Purchase
Fund; the Julia B. Engel Purchase fund; the Equitable Life
Assurance Society of the United States Purchase Fund; the
Sondra and Charles Gilman, Jr., Foundation, Inc.; S. Sidney
Kahn; The Lauder Foundation, Leonard and Evelyn Lauder Fund;
the Sara Roby Foundation; and the Painting and Sculpture
Committee

Index to Colorplates

1. *Flag*. 1954–1955.
Few works by Johns exist before this signature painting. He has done more than 20 paintings and numerous sculptures, drawings, and prints of flags—placed on larger fields, repeated in twos or threes, or aligned vertically.

2. *Target with Plaster Casts*. 1955.
Johns's first two Targets include plaster casts of parts of the body set into compartments with lids. Johns's subsequent Targets eliminate the Surrealist overtones created by these fragments of human anatomy and focus on the abstract geometry of the target's concentric circular design.

3. *Numbers in Color*. 1958–1959.
Johns's first Number paintings show individual numerals centered on rectangular fields. Johns next developed this motif in a series in which the digits 0 to 9 are arranged in a predetermined sequence that creates a complete, closed system. This painting is the most colorful version of these grids of stencilled numbers first done in monochromes of gray and white.

4. *False Start*. 1959.
Until this first major oil painting, Johns had used the wax-based medium of encaustic to create solid-looking, densely layered surfaces. Here, color names function visually like brush strokes. Some function as labels, but others present a paradoxical relationship between what is read and what is seen ("white" printed in red on yellow).

5. *Painting with Two Balls*. 1960.
This is one of the first works in which Johns uses the format of three horizontal registers. The title is an ironic pun on the idea—deeply engrained in the masculine mystique of Abstract Expressionism—that a good painting had to have "balls."

6. *Painted Bronze (Savarin Can)*. 1960.
This sculpture is completely cast in bronze and hand-painted by the artist. Its illusionism is so effective that initially it is hard to tell that it is not a Duchampian ready-made. The sculpture depicts objects that had made their way from Johns's kitchen to his studio, where they took on new functions as art tools used to store brushes and mix paints.

7. *Lands End*. 1963.
This painting belongs to a group of works from the early to mid-1960s with titles that refer to the seashore, including *By the Sea*, *Diver*, *Hatteras*, *Edisto*, and *Folly Beach*. The outstretched arm cuts across the picture space in an expressive gesture that may suggest a drowning figure, while the half circle scraped onto the surface with a stick calls attention to the activity of manipulating paint.

8. *Field Painting*. 1963–1964.
The central motif of this painting is the primary color names printed vertically in mirror-image letters. There are also three-dimensional wooden letters attached with hinges. The "R" of "Red" is made of neon tubing that lights up when the switch included in the painting is activated. Objects used to make the painting are attached to the letters by magnets.

9. *Decoy*. 1971.
All the motifs in *Decoy* derive from previous paintings, sculptures, lithographs, and etchings reworked into a complex, self-referential image. The work includes a zig-zag arrangement of color names, the legs derived from the upside-down figure in *Watchman* (fig. 2), and a photograph of the ale can used as a model for Johns's 1960 *Painted Bronze* (plate 6).

10. *Untitled*. 1972.
This large multipaneled painting includes images that are disturbingly disjunctive. The seven wax casts are taken from at least four different models. One fragment showing a hand and foot with a sock and a section of floorboards suggests a frozen moment in a narrative. The pattern at the left is painted in green, orange, and violet on a white ground with red, yellow, and blue showing through. Variations on this color scheme are used in many of Johns's crosshatchings abstractions from the next decade.

11. *Racing Thoughts*. 1983.
The setting for this autobiographical painting is Johns's bathroom in his Stony Point, New York, home. Besides the references to important figures in his life as an artist, Johns includes two pieces of pottery (one is by George Ohr, the eccentric ceramicist whose work Johns has collected; the other, a commemorative vase designed to read as silhouetted profiles).

12. *Untitled*. 1987.
In some variations on this motif faces are depicted on cloths that are nailed onto a wall; in others, the faces are on sheets of paper nailed or taped to the wall. The row of three hanging cloths may in part refer to Marcel Duchamp's *Bride Stripped Bare by Her Bachelors, Even*, specifically the area showing three irregular squares in a cloud representing the Bride's "cinematic blossoming."

13. *Fall*. 1986.
This painting is from a series named after the four seasons of the year that show the artist's shadow set in different locations where he has worked. Among his possessions are canvases that symbolize his artistic concerns. In *Fall* he includes Marcel Duchamp's self-portrait next to the skull and crossbones from *Racing Thoughts* (plate 11). At the bottom, where George Ohr's pottery tumbles out of the picture, the edge of a double flag appears.

14. *Green Angel*. 1990.
The cryptic image that dominates this painting is probably traced from an art source. Unlike Johns's earlier works based on familiar things, this figure's identity is so obscured that the mind cannot interpret it. In the many versions Johns has done, this cryptic form is nearly always placed amidst the eyes, nose, and lips of a woman's face that appears to gravitate toward the corners of the pictorial field.

15. *Untitled*. 1988.
This watercolor contains reference to the two modern masters who have most inspired and challenged his work. A copy of Pablo Picasso's *Straw Hat with Blue Leaf* (1936) done in reverse shows a sexually charged image that merges a distorted woman's face with a still-life composition. The background wall contains the image of Marcel Duchamp's *Bride* (1912), a reference to the erotic activities suggested by the bride and her bachelors in *Large Glass* (1915–1923).

1. *Flag*. 1954–1955. Encaustic, oil, and collage on fabric mounted on plywood, 42 ¼ x 60 ⅝".
Collection of The Museum of Modern Art, New York. Gift of Philip Johnson in honor of Alfred H. Barr, Jr.

2. *Target with Plaster Casts*. 1955. Encaustic on canvas with plaster cast objects. 51 x 44 x 3 ½".
Collection of Leo Castelli, New York

3. *Numbers in Color*. 1958–1959. Encaustic and collage on canvas, 66 ½ x 49 ¼".
Albright-Knox Art Gallery, Buffalo, New York. Gift of Seymour H. Knox, 1959

4. *False Start*. 1959. Oil on canvas, 67 ¼ x 54".
Collection of Mr. S. I. Newhouse, Jr.

5. *Painting with Two Balls*. 1960. Encaustic and collage on canvas with objects, 65 x 54".
Collection of the artist

6. *Painted Bronze.* 1960. 13 ½ x 8"diameter.
Collection of the artist

7. *Land's End*. 1963. Oil on canvas with objects, 67 x 48".
Collection of The San Francisco Museum of Modern Art. Gift of Mr. and Mrs. Harry W. Anderson

8. *Field Painting*. 1963–1964. Oil on canvas with objects, 72 x 36¾".
Collection of the artist

9. *Decoy*. 1971. Lithograph, 41½ x 29⁹⁄₁₆".
Universal Limited Art Editions, Inc., New York

10. *Untitled.* 1972. Oil, encaustic, and collage on canvas with objects, 72 x 192".
Collection of Museum Ludwig, Cologne

11. *Racing Thoughts*. 1983. Encaustic and collage on canvas, 48 x 75⅛".
Collection of The Whitney Museum of American Art. For complete information, see copyright page

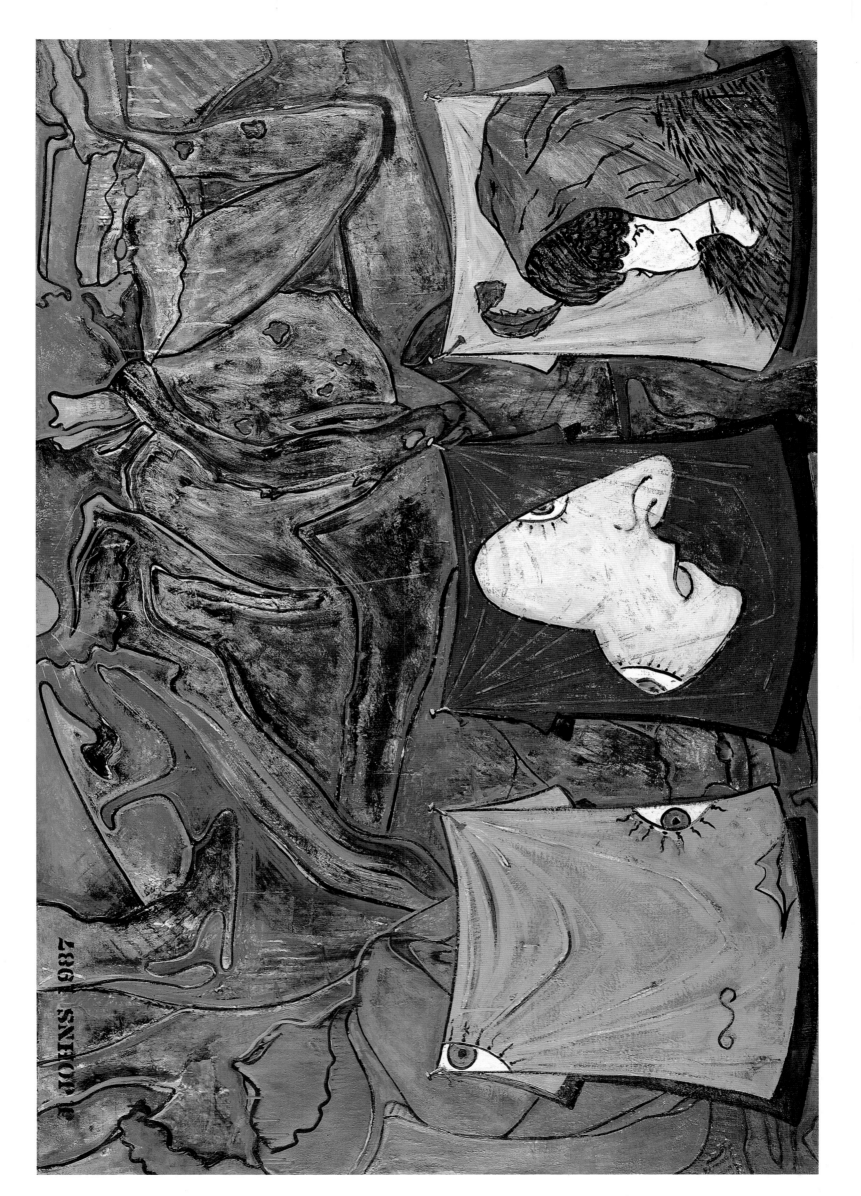

12. *Untitled*. 1987. Encaustic and collage on canvas, 50 x 75".
Collection of Robert and Jane Meyerhoff

13. *Fall*. 1986. Encaustic on canvas, 75 x 50".
Collection of the artist.

14. *Green Angel*. 1990. Encaustic and sand on canvas, 75 x 50".
Collection of the Walker Art Center, Minneapolis. In honor of Martin and Mildred Friedman, 1990

15. *Untitled*. 1988. Watercolor and pencil on paper, 21½ x 30".
Collection of Barbarlee Diamonstein and Carl Spielvogel